Free Soloing and Other
EXTREME ROCK CLIMBING

by Elliott Smith

Consultant: Daniel Lee
Outdoor Emergency Care Certified

CAPSTONE PRESS
a capstone imprint

Edge Books are published by Capstone Press
1710 Roe Crest Drive
North Mankato, Minnesota 56003
www.capstonepub.com

Library of Congress Cataloging-in-Publication Data is
available on the Library of Congress website.
ISBN 978-1-5435-7325-1 (library binding)
ISBN 978-1-5435-7331-2 (eBook PDF)

Editorial Credits
Anna Butzer, editor; Cynthia Della-Rovere, designer;
Kelly Garvin, media researcher;
Katy LaVigne, production specialist

Photo Credits
Alamy/Corey Rich/Aurora Photos/Cavan Images, 5, 7; Getty Images: Anne Ackermann, 11, Keith Ladzinski, cover
and back cover; iStockphoto: aluxum, 20, elnavegante, 27, Fertnig, 29, xavierarnau, 21; Newscom/Galen Rowell/
Mountain Light, 9; Shutterstock: klikkipetra, 19, Maciej Blesowski, 12, makasana photo, 13, Natalila Liubinetska,
16-17, PedkoAnton, 15, sss615, 25, Tom Grundy, 23
Design elements: Shutterstock: meunierd, pupsy

All internet sites appearing in back matter were available and accurate when this book was sent to press.

Printed and bound in the United States of America.
2644

Chapter 1
Hanging by His Fingertips. 4

Chapter 2
What is Free Solo? 8

Chapter 3
Trad Climbing 12

Visual Glossary 16

Chapter 4
Sport Climbing 18

Chapter 5
Bouldering 22

Chapter 6
Ice Climbing. 24

Chapter 7
How to Get Started 26

Glossary 30
Read More 31
Internet Sites. 31
Index .32

Fingertips

At more than 3,000 feet (914 meters) tall, El Capitan has been called a natural wonder of the world. Located in Yosemite National Park, El Capitan is one of the most popular hiking spots in the United States. Now, imagine climbing it without any equipment or safety gear! That's exactly what Alex Honnold did in 2017. He became the first person to ever complete a free solo climb of the entire face of El Capitan. This amazing feat took him less than four hours to finish. Any false step would have led to disaster. But Honnold made the ultimate challenge look easy.

Alex Honnold free solo climbs
The Nose on El Capitan in Yosemite
National Park, California.

Honnold climbed some of the world's toughest rocks to prepare for El Capitan. He had practiced his footwork and built his arm strength in the months before his attempt. Before the climb, he marked spots on the rock where he would make difficult holds and reaches. Starting just after dawn on June 3, 2017, Honnold began his climb. He had to squeeze his body into tight spaces and hang by his fingertips in some tricky sections. After he finished, Honnold sat on a lower rock formation, ate an apple, and enjoyed the natural beauty.

"Honestly, I think this is the most satisfied I've ever been," Honnold said in an interview afterward. "It was exactly what I hoped for. I felt so good. It went pretty much perfectly. Physically [the climb] is not that hard to execute. It's more you have to be in exactly the right [mental] place."

CHAPTER 2

What is Free Solo?

Free solo is a form of rock climbing in which there is no safety equipment used. Instead of a rope, harness, or other safety gear, an experienced climber moves alone. In addition, free solo climbs are usually performed at high **elevations**. While some rock face climbs are about 30 feet (9 m), most solo climbs are thousands of feet in the air. The rock face is the steep **vertical** surface of natural climbing face. Only the most experienced rock climbers consider free solo climbs.

While thrilling, these climbs have an extreme amount of risk. In no way should free solo be attempted by beginners. Even the most skilled climbers put in years of practice before attempting any free solo climbs.

Why would anyone try such a dangerous sport? Free solo climbers enjoy the freedom of being in nature without any equipment. Many free solo athletes say the experience is unlike any other climb. Even in the most dangerous of situations, athletes appreciate the natural beauty of their surroundings.

elevation—the height of the land above sea level
vertical—straight up and down

Speed is another key element of free solo. Climbs that can take days with equipment are reduced to hours when only hands and feet are used. Paths that use ropes and other equipment are not the most direct route to the top. But going free solo gives climbers a straighter approach to the **apex**.

Urban Free Solo

While most free solo climbers visit national parks or mountain ranges, some take a different path. Urban climbers explore the natural beauty of a city by climbing buildings!

Many urban climbers begin with rocks before moving on to massive towers. They use nothing more than their hands and feet to scale some of the world's tallest buildings. But do not attempt to climb a building. Only very experienced climbers tackle these difficult challenges. Climbers do have to get permission before they start their journeys. The Cayan Tower in Dubai and Willis Tower in Chicago are some of the structures urban free solo athletes strive to climb.

Urban free climbing is also called buildering.

Most free solo climbers rely on two key pieces of equipment: chalk and climbing shoes. Climbers carry a bag of chalk and use it to keep their hands dry. Since one slip could be the difference between success and a fall, this is a key element. The best sneakers allow climbers to stuff their toes into cracks while protecting their ankles from rocks.

Free solo can take place anywhere there's a willing climber and a rock formation. But some of the best locations include Bear's Reach in California and Separate Reality at Yosemite.

apex—the highest point of something

Staring up at a mountain can be scary, even for an experienced climber. But for those ready to conquer the rock, traditional climbing, or trad climbing, is a fun way to the top. Traditional climbing involves using gear placed in rock features to aid in climbing. The pieces are removed after the climb is finished, leaving the rock in its natural form.

Carabiners, cams, and chocks are all essential tools used while climbing.

Climbers must carry tools such as **chocks** and **cams** to place into cracks in the rock. They also use **slings** and **carabiners** to help secure ropes. They use these tools to create anchors to help them move up the rock. This kind of climbing works best in small groups. Partners can help offer advice during the climb and suggest which tools to use.

cam—a metal, spring-loaded piece of rock climbing protection equipment
carabiner—an oval-shaped metal clip; climbers use carabiners to secure rope to anchors
chock—a tapered metal wedge attached to a wire cable with a loop; a chock is wedged into cracks in rocks
sling—a tied or sewn loop of webbing used for protection during climbing

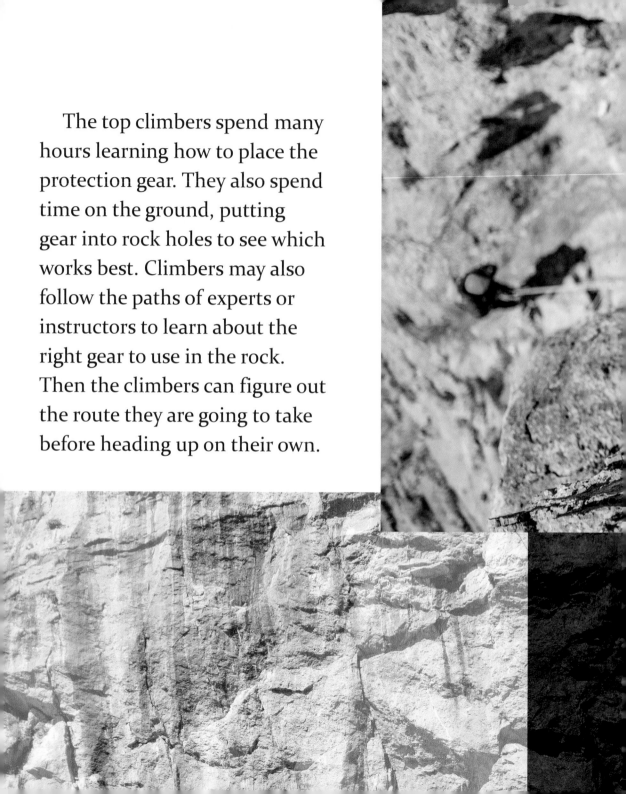

The top climbers spend many hours learning how to place the protection gear. They also spend time on the ground, putting gear into rock holes to see which works best. Climbers may also follow the paths of experts or instructors to learn about the right gear to use in the rock. Then the climbers can figure out the route they are going to take before heading up on their own.

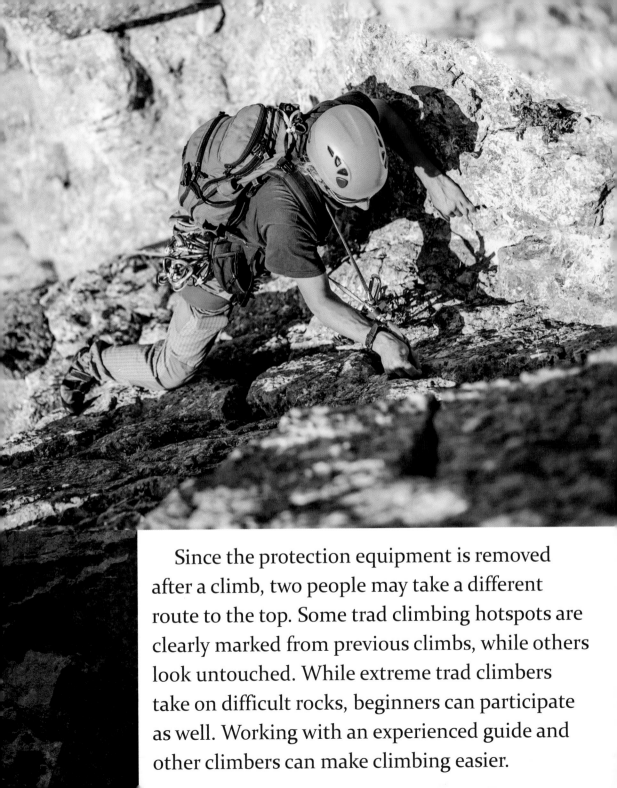

Since the protection equipment is removed after a climb, two people may take a different route to the top. Some trad climbing hotspots are clearly marked from previous climbs, while others look untouched. While extreme trad climbers take on difficult rocks, beginners can participate as well. Working with an experienced guide and other climbers can make climbing easier.

Visual Glossary

rope
There are two kinds of rope, dynamic and static. Dynamic rope is more elastic and used to absorb weight during a fall.

helmet
A climbing helmet is designed to protect the climber's head from any falling rock or debris.

rock climbing shoes
Climbing shoes protect the climber's feet while providing the friction needed to grip footholds.

chocks
These metal wedges are used for protection while climbing. They are placed in cracks and are less harmful to rock structures than other protection gear.

carabiners
Carabiners connect the climbing rope to pieces of climbing protection, such as bolts, nuts, and camming devices.

CHAPTER 4

Sport Climbing

Speed and strength are the major elements in sport climbing, which has grown in popularity recently. Sport climbing differs from traditional climbing in one major way. In traditional climbing, athletes use gear to create a route up the rock. In sport climbing, pre-placed bolts with metal hangers are attached to the rock. Climbers then clip into the hangers and make their way upward.

Pre-placed bolts help sport climbers focus on the physical challenge of a climb.

Sport climbing is designed to be a much more physical and competitive activity than traditional climbing. It is also more accessible because there is less gear and time involved. Sport routes are usually short distances, allowing climbers to complete difficult routes in one trip. The goal of sport climbing is to reach the top without falling or stopping to rest on a bolt. Experts in the sport push their bodies to the limit to achieve the fastest time.

In many ways, sport climbing is similar to gymnastics. Athletes practice the same routine over and over. That way, when they are at the rock, they can go as fast as possible. If they can successfully complete the route they've practiced, it's called a redpoint. Unlike other climbing sports, falling is not a major issue in sport climbing. Participants are attached to a rope and may fall several times while finishing difficult moves.

Indoor climbing walls allow athletes to practice their skills in a controlled environment.

Sport climbs are assigned ratings to help determine their difficulty. Climbs range from the easiest at 5.0 to the most difficult at 5.15. The rating is determined by the crux. The crux is the most difficult or hardest section of a climb. Trying to reach a difficult handhold or find a foot position on flat rock may be a crux. Many sport climbers first learn the **maneuvers** on indoor climbing walls before heading outside for tougher challenges.

maneuver—a planned and controlled movement that requires practiced skills

CHAPTER 5

Bouldering

Bouldering is a simple but challenging sport that requires little equipment and offers lots of fun. Athletes try to complete different bouldering routes, which are called problems. Unlike free solo, which also doesn't use ropes or harnesses, bouldering is much safer. Most routes are less than 20 feet (6.1 m) tall, and crash pads are often used for safety. In addition, bouldering sites don't require athletes to travel to **remote** locations. All that's needed is a challenging rock to climb.

Highball Bouldering

The most extreme form of bouldering is called highball. Climbers make their way over large rocks without any safety equipment. The range for highball is between 15 to 40 feet (4.6 to 12.2 m) and is reserved for skilled climbers. Highball began in 1961 with the climb of a 37-foot (11.3-m) boulder called The Thimble, in South Dakota.

Since then, extreme climbers have been searching for bigger boulders to scale. Some of the biggest climbs include boulders as big as 55 feet (16.8 m). Those numbers nearly reach the top of the V-Scale, which was established to rate bouldering routes. Highball climbers use very large crash pads to cushion falls.

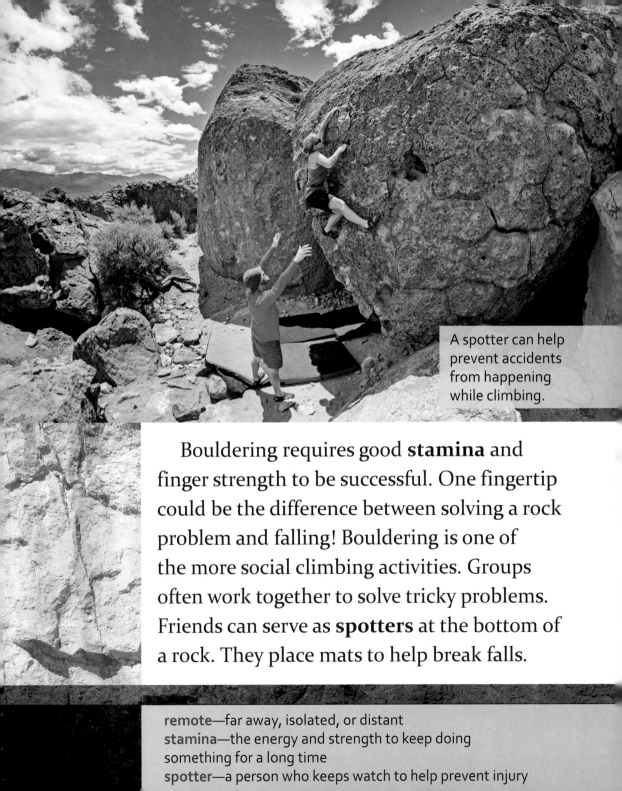

A spotter can help prevent accidents from happening while climbing.

Bouldering requires good **stamina** and finger strength to be successful. One fingertip could be the difference between solving a rock problem and falling! Bouldering is one of the more social climbing activities. Groups often work together to solve tricky problems. Friends can serve as **spotters** at the bottom of a rock. They place mats to help break falls.

remote—far away, isolated, or distant
stamina—the energy and strength to keep doing something for a long time
spotter—a person who keeps watch to help prevent injury

CHAPTER 6

Ice Climbing

Ice climbing, sometimes called mountaineering, puts a frosty spin on natural fun. But it's not quite as simple as waiting for the weather to get cold before climbing. There are several types of ice that climbers prefer, each leading to different experiences and challenges.

Alpine ice is created from old snow and is hard-packed into ice. This kind of ice can be steep and usually results in long, slippery routes. Water ice is created by runoff and can lead to bumps, ridges, and icicles. Those features make climbing water ice more difficult.

Ice climbing calls for unique tools. Crampons are special traction devices attached to shoes. They help dig into the snow and ice and make walking easier. Ice axes are used to move up the mountain. An ice climber can swing an axe and dig it into the ice to climb. Climbers also use ice screws to clip into on their way up the mountain.

CHAPTER 7

How to Get Started

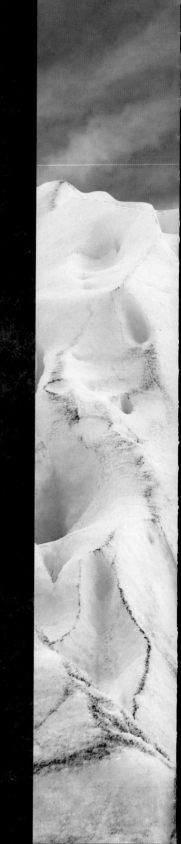

Extreme climbing is an awesome outdoor activity with an up-close view of nature. While free solo is off-limits for beginning climbers, learning the basics of climbing is not. All the proper safety steps must be taken. Young climbers should never go off alone. Proper equipment must be used at all times.

Young climbers can use indoor or outdoor climbing facilities to get started. Some beginners go to indoor climbing gyms to learn simple moves before heading outside. And while climbing rocks may seem scary, a guide can provide the tips needed to succeed.

Ice climbers scale a glacier in Argentina.

Don't be afraid to start small. Bouldering is a great first step for young climbers, as long as spotters are involved. Young climbers should start off using a harness. Some harnesses are made of two pieces, giving kids room to grow. Ripstop pants are durable bottoms that protect climbers from scrapes and bumps on rocks. And while climbing helmets are available, a sturdy bike helmet can also be used for this sport.

Climbing is a fantastic way to get outdoors and be healthy. Grab an adult and some friends and explore this exciting sport together.

Glossary

apex (AY-peks)—the highest point of something

cam (KAM)—a metal, spring-loaded piece of rock climbing protection equipment

carabiner (kar-uh-BEE-nuhr)—an oval-shaped metal clip; climbers use carabiners to secure rope to anchors

chock (CHAHK)—a tapered metal wedge attached to a wire cable with a loop; a chock is wedged into cracks in rocks

elevation (e-luh-VAY-shuhn)—the height of the land above sea level

maneuver (muh-NOO-ver)—a planned and controlled movement that requires practiced skills

remote (ri-MOHT)—far away, isolated, or distant

sling (SLING)—a tied or sewn loop of webbing used for protection during climbing

spotter (SPOT-uhr)—a person who keeps watch to help prevent injury

stamina (STAM-uh-nuh)—the energy and strength to keep doing something for a long time

vertical (VUR-tuh-kuhl)—straight up and down

Read More

Bramucci, Steve. *Rock Stars!* National Geographic Kids. Washington, D.C.: National Geographic Kids, 2018

Doeden, Matt. *Can You Survive Extreme Mountain Climbing?* You Choose: Survival. North Mankato, MN: Capstone Press, 2012.

Dugan, Christine. *Rock Climbing.* Defying Gravity! Huntington Beach, CA: Teacher Created Materials, 2012.

Internet Sites

The Mountaineers: Kids Programs
https://www.mountaineers.org/youth/kids-programs

USA Climbing:
http://www.usaclimbing.org/

INDEX

apex, 10

bouldering, 22, 23, 28

crash pads, 22
cruxes, 21

dangers, 8, 9

El Capitan, 4, 6
equipment, 4, 8, 9, 10, 11, 12,
   13, 14, 15, 16, 17, 18, 19, 20,
   22, 23, 25, 26, 28

free solo, 4, 8, 9, 10, 11, 22, 26

highball, 22
Honnold, Alex, 4, 6

ice climbing, 24, 25
indoor climbing walls, 21, 26

nature, 6, 9, 26

practice, 6, 8, 10, 14, 20, 21, 26

ratings, 21, 22
redpoints, 20
routes, 14, 15, 18, 19, 20, 22, 24

speed, 10, 18, 19, 20, 24
sport climbing, 18, 19, 20, 21
spotters, 23, 28
strength, 6, 18, 23

traditional climbing, 12, 13, 14,
   15, 18, 19

urban climbing, 10

Yosemite National Park, 4, 11